so many doors

so many doors
Celia McBride

Playwrights Canada Press
Toronto

PLAYWRIGHTS CANADA PRESS
The Canadian Drama Publisher
215 Spadina Ave., Suite 230, Toronto, ON Canada M5T 2C7
phone 416.703.0013 fax 416.408.3402
orders@playwrightscanada.com • www.playwrightscanada.com

Playwrights Canada Press acknowledges the financial support of the Government of Canada through the Canada Book Fund and the Canada Council for the Arts and the Province of Ontario through the Ontario Arts Council and the Ontario Media Development Corporation for our publishing activities.

 Canada Council for the Arts   Conseil des Arts du Canada   ONTARIO ARTS COUNCIL CONSEIL DES ARTS DE L'ONTARIO

 Canada   Ontario
Ontario Media Development Corporation

Cover image © Niels Timmer
Cover and type design by Blake Sproule

LIBRARY AND ARCHIVES CANADA CATALOGUING IN PUBLICATION

McBride, Celia
So many doors / Celia McBride.

Play.
Also available in electronic format.
ISBN 978-0-88754-921-2

I. Title.

PS8625.C34S6 2010   C812'.6   C2010-905806-2

First edition: October 2010
Printed and bound in Canada by Canadian Printco, Scarborough

For the parents.

I was very happy to go and work in the Yukon on Celia's beautiful play. It was wonderful to workshop and premiere this work, born and bred in the Far North, and finally to share it with audiences all across the country.

What attracted me about this piece was its humanity—the depth and honesty with which Celia has realized these characters. Admittedly, this is tough material but it is also deeply cathartic.

So Many Doors is not so much a play about children who have passed as it is about those who are left behind to grieve, irrevocably damaged and faced with the arduous task of moving on. It is about both darkness and light but mostly it is about renewal and how, ultimately and inevitably, the process of letting go of someone involves facing ourselves.

—Kelly Thornton
Director/Dramaturg

Playwright's Notes

So Many Doors did not start out as a play about grieving parents. The original idea for the play needed higher stakes and in a sudden flash I envisioned two couples reunited by the death of their kids. A few days later a family in Whitehorse experienced the devastating loss of a very young child. A couple of days after that, both CBC Radio and the *Globe and Mail* featured stories about parents whose children had died. I was a little freaked out. I felt like I was getting very clear signals to either back off or write this play NOW. It soon became clear what I was meant to do.

This is a play about healing. Some of us get there and some of us don't. Who knows why? This is the Great Mystery. Many of us believe we do not deserve to recover. It's easier to believe we are supposed to suffer and that we are being punished. The hope lies in the possibility of change. We can let go and be reborn. We can be healed and rediscover the joy of being alive. Like Shay, all we have to do is raise our hand and say, "I'll go," and then share our pain, speak our truth, and let the healing begin.

Notes on the Script

Lines said by ALL FOUR are not necessarily said in unison.
LINEE is pronounced lin-EE.

The premiere of *So Many Doors* was co-produced by Sour Brides Theatre, Nakai Theatre, and the Yukon Arts Centre in Whitehorse, Yukon, in October 2007 with the following cast:

Jed   Derek Metz*
Linee   Moira Sauer
Lyle   Corey Turner*
Shay   Celia McBride

Directed and dramaturged by Kelly Thornton
Designed by David Skelton
Music and sound by Andrea McColeman
Stage managed by Jenny Hamilton
Production coordination by Katherine McCallum

The production was remounted for the Magnetic North Theatre Festival in Vancouver, BC, in June 2008 with the same cast as above.

The following cast appeared in the Yukon remount in January 2009 and the ensuing national tour to Ontario, New Brunswick, and the Northwest Territories:

Jed   Brett Watson*
Linee   Moira Sauer
Lyle   Jesse Todd*
Shay   Celia McBride

Directed and dramaturged by Kelly Thornton
Lighting by Cimmeron Meyer
Costumes by Linda Talbot
Music and sound by Andrea McColeman
Stage managed by Melania Radelicki
Ontario production management by Cimmeron Meyer
New Brunswick production Management by Kirsten Watt
Northwest Territories production management by Dean Eyre

* Appeared courtesy of the Canadian Actors' Equity Association

Death hath so many doors to let out life.
　—John Fletcher (1579–1625)

Characters

Jed
Linee
Lyle
Shay

Lights up on SHAY, LYLE, JED, *and* LINEE.

SHAY   I don't know what to say. We're supposed to talk but I don't know what to say. Lyle thinks talking about it to a room full of people is going to make a difference but I don't. It's nobody's business. If he wants to deal with it by talking then fine, that's his thing. Why do we have to do everything together? If they ask me to talk, I'm just going to pass. It's bad enough that we have to sit here with Jed and Linee let alone share our most private feelings.

LYLE   We've all been through the same thing. We're connected by it.

LINEE   I know I need to be here. I can't speak for anyone else but this helps me. It helps me to not blow my brains out, basically.

JED   It's a shot in the dark as far as I'm concerned. I've never been one for the touchy-feely stuff. Can you feel the love tonight and all that. Christ.

SHAY   I just stare at the floor and wait.

LYLE   This thing… y'know, it's every parent's worst nightmare. Ya hear it all the time. "Every parent's worst nightmare." And when it happens to you… ya can't believe it. And it's true, yer whole world changes. Not in the way you think, I mean, yeah, obviously nothin' will ever be the same again a-course but… it's like… the buildin's you been starin' at your whole life don't look like the same buildin's anymore. Colours are… they're not the same colours. It's like you've woken up on some other planet somewhere. Some new planet where your kid doesn't exist. You were on this other planet and… you had a kid. Then somethin' happened and… now you don't. See, Carol-Anne—

SHAY   Don't say her name.

LYLE   She doesn't want me to say her name.

SHAY   Lyle is so good. He's so good and sometimes… it just makes me want to be bad.

JED   The days pass. You wake up, you go to work. You have to. You don't have a choice. The world doesn't stop for you. It turns and you either get on for the ride or you don't.

LINEE   Yeah, I did have that thought. I'll admit it. I thought God was punishing me. I kept wondering what the hell I did to deserve the life I suddenly had, which had started out really good, by the way. But living with Jed's drinking had become a total torture. I felt like I was serving a life sentence. I was asking "Why me?" all the time and feeling so sorry for myself. And then when the accident happened and Jed Jr. died I felt like I got sent to death row. I couldn't understand it. I kept trying to figure out what I'd done wrong. Why is this happening to me? What did I do to deserve this? Why am I being punished? I needed something to explain it.

SHAY   "God doesn't make bad things happen, God is *there for you* when bad things happen." Well, I am here to protest that notion. I am here to *protest that*.

LYLE   The evenings can be rough. Shay started watchin' TV at night and it's pretty much all she does now. We used to walk the property or take the horses out, y'know? Go ridin'. Now she just lies on the couch watchin' all these shows. Crime shows and stuff. Just grim. I can't watch them things. But I managed to convince her to come to this group. I kinda had to break her down, ask her to do it for me, for us, y'know? And even if nothin' comes out of it… at least she's gettin' outta the house and away from the TV once a week.

LINEE	The thing about Group is we all share this common bond and unless you've been through something like this yourself you can't ever really understand it. It's not therapy. It's support.
LYLE	I like it how everybody just listens. Gettin' through it together. There's some even got to find some peace around it. And I'm headin' for that. I want the peace.
SHAY	I just want it to be over. I just want it to end. I just want the end of this.
JED	You see… the important thing to remember is this: the important thing to remember is—and I always say this—because it's the most important thing and that is… when you're living in the kind of world we live in today, the kind of world where… where something unexpected can happen and… and why would you? Why would you expect that on a sunny afternoon in early winter a guy in a truck would… would hit a patch of ice on the road and lose control and… and side-swipe a… a… a christ, a… a daycare worker pushing a double stroller and… and you're suddenly—you know… you don't know but… but the one thing you need to remember is that… that… when something like this happens—and who's to blame? You can't do well to blame anybody because it's nobody's fault! You think it's your fault. You think, "Why did we pick that goddamn particular daycare?" There were a christ of a dozen others or… "If only we hadn't taken him in that day," and on and on and hey, I'm not trying to sound like any kind of expert here because I'm no goddamn expert but I do think that the most important thing to remember is that… christ… see I never expected to be here. I just never… expected to be… here.

Lights change. LINEE and SHAY at Group.

LINEE	Hi.
SHAY	Hello.
LINEE	You came back. Is it just you tonight?
SHAY	Lyle's coming.

LINEE   You guys left so fast last week I thought we'd never see you again. *(pause)* I know you still hate me but I'm really, really glad you're here.

Lights change. SHAY, LINEE, LYLE, *and* JED.

SHAY   They're a form of torture. Support groups.

LYLE   It's an hour a week. I told her it's not gonna kill her.

LINEE   I've been coming for six months and already I've started to see all these events in my life, all these things that have happened, including the things that felt like hell on earth... I see them as connected now. They've all kind of merged together to carry me here, to this place where I'm at now. All these things, like the fact that Shay and I knew each other Back East and then we both ended up here and then we got pregnant at the same time and gave birth at the same time. It sounds like coincidence but then when J.J. and Carol-Anne both died in the same accident? It's too much to be a—to not be... something more. Now we've all ended up in Group? After not speaking to each other for three years? It has to be something more.

JED   The papers called it a coincidence.

LYLE   "Sad coincidence for local best friends."

SHAY   They got the best friends part wrong.

LINEE   How many times does a person have to say they're sorry?

LYLE   We did have a good thing goin' there for a while. We had a good time.

JED   Yeah, we did.

SHAY   Torture.

Lights change. LINEE *and* SHAY *at Group.*

LINEE   I had this bad pain in my chest? Like a hundred-pound weight
           pressing on me and it was killing me. And it's gone now.
           Seriously, I know it sounds stupid but after about a month of
           coming here it just went away. I mean, I know it was anxiety,
           obviously, but I tried everything short of jumping in the river
           to have it just stop. All of a sudden I could breathe again 'cause
           I was finally getting all this garbage out.

           JED enters, jovial. It's obvious he's been drinking.

JED   I thought I was late.

LINEE   You are, we haven't started yet.

JED   Shayla, Linee told me you guys showed up last week. It's good
           to see you.

SHAY   Jed.

JED   Lyle here?

SHAY   He's on his way.

JED   Okay, do I have time to go to the john?

LINEE   Hurry.

JED   You're looking great. This is great.

           LYLE enters.

           Lyle! Christ.

           JED hugs him.

LYLE   Jedi, how's it goin'?

JED   It's good, good. I'll be right back, I'm...

           He exits. LYLE kisses SHAY.

LINEE	Hi, Lyle.
LYLE	Hello, Linee. How are ya?
LINEE	Doin' well. How are you?
LYLE	Not bad, not bad. We the only ones tonight?
LINEE	Might be. Sometimes people don't come till quarter after. It varies from week to week.
LYLE	Oh yeah.
LINEE	Sue and Jake come pretty regularly. There's a woman whose eight-year-old daughter died of cancer, she comes sometimes. Audrey Glazer, you know Audrey, she wasn't here last week but she does come. There are one or two others that come on and off. Sometimes it's just me. Jed only came tonight to see you.
LYLE	Yeah, well. That's all right. It's been a while, eh?
LINEE	I didn't think you guys would come back.
LYLE	We figured one time wasn't enough to know, y'know?
LINEE	It's not, really.
	Silence.
LYLE	'S gettin' colder out there. Wind's pickin' up.
LINEE	Don't say that.
LYLE	Callin' for snow tonight.
LINEE	Be quiet.
LYLE	S'posed to go down to minus fifteen.
LINEE	Shh.

LYLE	What.
LINEE	Don't say "minus."
LYLE	Won't last. S'posed to go back up to five or six by the weekend.
LINEE	Okay, you can talk about that.

She laughs.

LYLE	Global warmin'.
LINEE	I'm all for it.
LYLE	Say by 2025 or so it's gonna be like the tropics up here.
LINEE	Well, it was plus six yesterday, it felt like plus twenty in our yard. I was outside in the back and the sun was shining and I had a T-shirt on, it was gorgeous. I know it's early. I know it's impossible that spring could be here and I'm going to get burned—I always do—but God I just love the light coming back, it's so reassuring, hey? The change is so dramatic at this time of year. Winter's on its way out.

JED re-enters and touches SHAY.

JED	Christ, this is great.

He slaps LYLE on the back.

How're you doing? How's the business?

LYLE	Can't complain. Keepin' our heads above water anyway.
JED	I hear you're keeping them higher than that.
LYLE	We had a decent winter. Shay's good with the books.
JED	Shayla. Christ, it's great to see you guys!
ALL FOUR	How the hell did we get here?

Lights change. SHAY *and* LYLE *on their ranch.*

SHAY   I met Lyle in a hotel bar Down South. It's all Down South up here even if it's Back East. And it doesn't matter which city, it's all the Big City. So there I was, living in the Big City Down South Back East and Lyle had come down to take part in some entrepreneur's conference. He was staying in this hotel where I was waiting for a client. And he sat down right next to me and started chatting me up. I know how to get rid of men fast but Lyle... I didn't want to get rid of him. He was such a hick. But I liked it. It made me want to be honest with him. So I told him I worked for an escort service. He said:

SHAY & LYLE Like a high-class hooker?

SHAY   I told him I only had sex with the ones I liked. I told him I was putting myself through school. He said:

SHAY & LYLE Yer an entrepreneur just like me.

SHAY   And when my client arrived he plucked the flower from the old man's lapel and said:

LYLE   How 'bout you come back with me and we put our heads together and make some real money?

SHAY   This dorky guy from north of 60. I laughed at him. But I called him that night. He'd told me his room number.

LYLE   Twelve-forty-seven. Rhymes with I-just-met-a-woman-and-I-found-my-heaven.

SHAY   We talked on the phone for five hours. He was tender. His sincerity was something I didn't believe in people. I told him I couldn't go with him—that I had to finish university—and he said:

SHAY & LYLE Yes, you sure do.

SHAY   But he said he'd pay for my flight when I was done. And he did. It was February when I arrived. Pitch black at four-thirty in the afternoon and minus thirty-two. I almost didn't get off the plane. But Lyle was there, waiting for me. And he looked so cute in his big fur hat and parka we practically attacked each other.

LYLE   Born and raised here. This is home. Where else would a guy wanna live? Mountains. Good people. Laid back. Pace is right. Me and Shay got our hands in all kinds a different business now. Real estate, construction. Shay keeps the books and manages things, ya know? She's got a great mind for makin' money. She's got all these great ideas and how ta execute 'em. We work hard. And we do good. Got a nice place outside-a town. Buncha land. I saw it in her, y'know? I mean, she was there in that hotel bar waitin' for some jackass but that's not what I saw. I saw a hard worker.

SHAY   Only Lyle would look at a high-class hooker and see a hard worker.

She exits.

LYLE   Yeah, it bothers me. 'Course it does. Thinkin'a her with a bunch-a crusty ol' fat-cat jerkoffs… It makes me crazy if I really let myself think about it. I gotta turn it around. Look at her determination instead, y'know? She wanted a degree and she wanted a certain lifestyle for herself and she didn't wanna work for some fast-food-slave minimum wage, ya know? And she's estranged from her family so you know, she didn't have that support. It was business. And the bottom line is… she came to me. She came home… to me.

She re-enters.

SHAY   I never thought I'd stay. I told myself three months. I was taking a big chance on Lyle. Coming up here. It could have all blown up in my face. But I found myself wanting to make him happy. I wanted to please him. We got so we could afford to have someone iron his shirts and clean our house but I cooked him good meals and I learned to take care of the horses. I wanted to see the business work and I wanted us to be a success.

LYLE   We didn't tell no one how we met. People talk, ya know? She had to work hard at fittin' in. It's one-a these places... ya either love it or ya hate it.

SHAY   I found myself seduced by the light. The mountains on all sides of us, out of every window in our home like sleeping giants. I'd drive into town and catch myself slowing down to get a better look at the way the sun was hitting the peaks. This place... I'm telling you... it gets right down into the cracks of you. Even if you do leave you're always thinking about when you're going to come back.

LYLE   I'm ready to have a family again but it's been harder on Shay, y'know? I thought if we got some kinda help... maybe she'd come around.

Lights change. LINEE and JED in their house.

LINEE   Jed and I met at this huge party after we'd both just graduated from university. We were both plastered and it sure felt like love at first sight. We both really believed we'd found the one. Our families were devastated when we told them we'd gotten married in Las Vegas. We actually did that. We drove down with a bunch of our crazy friends and got hitched in Vegas.

JED   Christ, we had a lot of laughs on that trip.

LINEE   As soon as we got back the buzz started to wear off. So Jed started looking for another adventure. He said:

LINEE & JED   Let's go to the Far North.

JED   I was talking to this friend of mine who'd spent a summer here and he told me how easy it was to get a government job and we just decided to go for it. I managed to convince Linee she'd be able to get a teaching job no problem, so we up and left.

LINEE   You could say I wasn't exactly thinking clearly. I hate the cold. I hate the dark. But I was so gaga at that point in our relationship I would have said yes to anything.

| JED | We drove across the country. We didn't have anything but the car and a couple of sleeping bags. Record collection. We were renegades. We stopped in all these tourist places on the way taking pictures of everything and laughing at people, stuff like that. We got along. We really had a good time. |

| LINEE | We drank a lot. I was the good-time gal. He was the clown. |

| JED | I liked it up here right away. It was different in a lot of ways that appealed to me. It's a small town with a city sense about it. Linee and Shay were friends. Lyle started to take me out hunting and fishing. I went nuts for the scenery. There's some views even in town that'll blow your mind apart. The cold isn't too bad. Christ, anywhere in this country's a hard winter. |

| LINEE | I started to drink less and Jed started to drink more. We stopped going out together and he stopped coming home. The winters started to get to me. Every year, as soon as the light started to disappear I'd think I'm not gonna make it. You're suddenly plunged into this darkness and I felt myself going right down with it. Every year it got worse. Jed kept saying: |

| LINEE & JED | You'll get used to it. |

| LINEE | I think if it hadn't been for Shay and Lyle I would have left. Just having that connection made staying easier. |

| JED | I started calling the rest of the world "Outside" as if I'd been here all my life. And it is like that. Outside. Inside. It's like living in an isolation booth. And Lyle says it's changing, and it's not what it used to be, but no matter how many big-box stores you get, no matter what the population increase is, you still have to drive for days to get out of here if the planes are grounded. There's still that distance separating us from the rest of the country. |

| LINEE | I think about leaving all the time. |

| JED | I want to die here. Bury me on a mountain someplace. |

Lights change. LINEE alone.

LINEE	I was totally floored to find out Shay was living up here. We hadn't been really close in high school but we became best friends pretty quick once we reconnected. After high school I kept hearing through the grapevine that she was working for an escort service. When we finally got up enough guts to ask her about it she was totally matter-of-fact about the whole thing.

LYLE enters.

LYLE	We asked 'em to keep it between the four of us, y'know? Jed and Linee… they respected that. For a good while anyway.

SHAY enters.

SHAY	Then I got pregnant.

LINEE	Jed and I had been trying to have a baby.

LYLE	I don't think Linee is really that kinda person, ya know? But it didn't make a helluva lotta sense.

LINEE	I had too much to drink.

JED enters.

JED	It was a christ-awful thing to do.

SHAY	She just blurted it out to a room full of people at a fancy fundraising party.

LINEE	"And now I'd like to welcome to the podium our very own Happy Hooker…!"

SHAY leaves.

I apologized about three million times. I practically got down on my hands and knees. Then I found out I was pregnant, like, two weeks later and she still wouldn't answer my calls.

LYLE	She can be stubborn.

JED	It was brutal.
LINEE	The pregnancy brought Jed and I back together in a way. We were both excited about having a kid. He became really affectionate and loving towards me. I started to feel like maybe there was something between us after all. Something we'd just needed time to discover.
JED	I don't know what it was. I guess I liked the idea. Never thought I wanted kids but... I started to see myself as a dad and... it made me feel good.

SHAY re-enters.

SHAY	I thought I'd be a terrible mother. My family's all messed up and I was scared I'd mess up the kid.
LYLE	She was a natural. It changed her. I mean... she became... open. So full-a love, ya know?
LINEE	Jed tried really hard, he really did. But after we lost J.J. he went right back to his old self.
JED	We didn't lose J.J. We didn't misplace him. It's a christ-awful expression.
LYLE	Acceptin' it's the hardest thing. I don't know if ya ever do.
LINEE	Jed Jr. and Carol-Anne ended up being born within a month of each other. I mean, how amazing is that? Really. Having our babies at almost exactly the same time? We could have shared so many things. But it was like I was dead to her.
SHAY	I'll do my duty as a wife and I'll support Lyle by coming to this group. I'll even sit next to her and make small talk because I know how to be polite. But I will not talk. I will not say a word.

Lights change. LYLE and JED at Group.

JED	Brother Lyle.

LYLE	Jedi. Haven't seen you here for a couple-a weeks—where you been?
JED	It's like this: if I come every three weeks Linee doesn't harass me about it and I can pretty much keep her from taking off on me.
LYLE	So you're not gettin' anythin' outta this?
JED	Not really. Are you?
LYLE	Startin' to. Yeah. I think so.
JED	Really? I thought Shayla'd been dragging you in here every week.
LYLE	I been the one draggin' her. She hates it.
JED	Does she? Huh. So she's not coming tonight?
LYLE	Yeah, no, she is. She'll be here.
JED	Christ, you know on one hand it's like nothing happened and it's normal to be talking to you and yet—
LYLE	Yeah, I know. I'm sorry about it. All that, y'know?
JED	You're sorry. I haven't been fishing in three years.
LYLE	You didn't need me to go fishin'.
JED	Are you kidding me?
LYLE	Yeah, yeah.
JED	You think I'm joking.

Silence.

Yeah, pretty nuts though, isn't it? This?

LYLE	Yeah, it's nuts all right. You ever pass by there?
JED	What, the daycare?
LYLE	Yeah.
JED	Not too often, no.
LYLE	I passed by there today goin' to the house—
JED	What house?
LYLE	Shay and I bought a house there and we're rentin' it out—
JED	What's that, like six houses you guys own now?
LYLE	I'm not at liberty to say.
JED	You're not at liberty to say. You're a dog.
LYLE	Anyways, I passed by the daycare and… there was a fresh bouquet of flowers tacked to the fence.
JED	That's what's her name doing that.
LYLE	Suba, yeah.
JED	Suba. Christ.
LYLE	I understand it though, y'know? Her bein' the one pushin' the stroller and everything—
JED	I know but it's like you get one good day where maybe you haven't thought about it so far, or if you have, it just passed through and you managed maybe not to dwell on it and then bam! You have to drive by a christing fresh bouquet of flowers hammered to the fence—
LYLE	That's the thing… today… I didn't mind seein' it so much, y'know?

JED	Christ, I can't stand it. I can't drive by there. It drives me nuts.
LYLE	*(pause)* It's good to talk about it.
JED	Linee talks about it all the time. She read somewhere it's supposed to help you if you bring him into the conversation and everything so she's always talking about him now.
LYLE	Me and Shay need to do that.
JED	I don't know, man. I kinda liked it better when we didn't.
LYLE	It's like starvin' yourself to death or somethin'. Not talkin' about it.
JED	Yeah, well, I didn't say we talked about it. It's more like she talks at me and I pretend I'm listening.
LYLE	You guys aren't really thinkin' of splittin' up, are ya?
JED	I'm not. She is. Christ, we already have in a way. I mean we live together but we're like roommates or something. Worse than that, we're like roommates who don't get along.
LYLE	Roommates. So...
JED	I sleep on the couch, man.
LYLE	Really, eh? So... what, you guys aren't doin' it anymore?
JED	It's rare.
LYLE	Rare, huh?
JED	It's more rare than steak tartare.
LYLE	I'm glad to hear we're not the only ones.
JED	You guys, too? Huh.

LYLE   Yeah. She's all shut down.

JED   Yeah? Wow. Huh.

LYLE   I'm lettin' her go through it, y'know, whatever she needs but…
         yeah. Takes time.

JED   Yeah. Huh.

         SHAY enters.

LYLE   Hey, baby.

         He kisses her. She sits next to JED.

JED   Hello, Shayla.

SHAY   Hi.

LYLE   Did you feed the dogs?

SHAY   The dogs, the cats, the chickens, the horses, and the donkey.

JED   You guys got a donkey?

SHAY   Birthday present.

LYLE   She loves that donkey!

SHAY   I do not.

LYLE   She loves him. Named him George Clooney.

SHAY   I did not.

LYLE   Now she can ride George Clooney whenever she wants.

         The guys crack up.

SHAY   It's such a bad joke.

LYLE	Everybody else thinks it's funny.

Lights change. End of Group. Everyone except SHAY is clapping.

JED	You don't say much.
SHAY	Neither do you.
JED	I talked.

LINEE joins them.

LINEE	Jed, who were you talking about? Mike...
JED	You don't know him.
LINEE	Obviously, that's why I'm asking you who he is.
JED	Mike McDonagh.
LINEE	I know him.
JED	You do not.
LINEE	I do so. He swims at the pool.
JED	Mike McDonagh does not swim at the pool.
LINEE	Yes, he does. Mike McDonagh swims at the pool, I see him every morning—
JED	Mike McDonald. Mike McDonald swims at the pool. You don't have to know everybody.
LINEE	I know I don't have to know everybody—
JED	So you don't know Mike McDonagh.
LINEE	Fine. Are you coming home—?
JED	Lyle? Drink?

LYLE	Can't tonight. Gotta get up at four tomorrow.
JED	Christ. Four?
SHAY	*(to LYLE)* Can we go?

Lights change. JED alone at Group. SHAY enters.

JED	No one here.
SHAY	I'm here.
JED	I meant—
SHAY	Lyle had to go out to the Cutoff. Cabin roof caved in.
JED	Yeah, this warm weather's nuts.
SHAY	Isn't Linee coming?
JED	I don't think so. She left me a message about some emergency board meeting or other.
SHAY	Do you think anyone else will come?
JED	It's five past.
SHAY	I'm gonna go.
JED	Oh, okay, yeah. Or… do you wanna go somewhere else?
SHAY	For what?
JED	I don't know, go for a drink or something.
SHAY	Oh.
JED	Christ, now that we're all talking again—
SHAY	Okay.

JED	Yeah?

Lights change. JED and SHAY in a bar.

SHAY	God, I'm so glad no one showed up tonight.
JED	You really can't stand it.
SHAY	I'm only going to support Lyle.
JED	Yeah, me too. Hey, you smiled.
SHAY	No, I didn't.
JED	It's good to see you out.
SHAY	I haven't been out in so long.
JED	It's great to see you.
SHAY	I look like a sack of rags.
JED	You look great.
SHAY	I do not.
JED	You always look good.

Silence.

It's pretty quiet in here. Do you want to go somewhere else?

SHAY	This is fine.
JED	Lyle said you guys bought another house.
SHAY	Did he?
JED	So what's that you got now, five, six houses and like a thousand acres?

SHAY   Yeah.

JED   You're a really good conversationalist, you know that?

SHAY   That's not a very nice thing to say.

JED   I'm only teasing you.

SHAY   I don't like being teased.

JED   I'm joking. Come on. This four-year gap thing is killing me—

SHAY   Three.

JED   Right.

SHAY   Everyone always wants to know how much money we have. I hate this town for that.

JED   I don't care about your money.

SHAY   So why did you ask?

JED   Because I'm trying to talk to you. Jesus.

SHAY   There has to be something else for us to talk about.

JED   Okay. Politics.

SHAY   No.

JED   Sports.

SHAY   Definitely no.

JED   Cooking?

SHAY   Cooking's good.

JED	Okay, ahhhhh... what's that thing you used to cook all the time for us? The chicken thing? With the thousand cloves of garlic or whatever?
SHAY	Forty.
JED	Was it only forty? Christ that was good. I really miss coming out to your place.
SHAY	Well, you should come out.
JED	Drinking wine from your cellar. Going into the bush with the horses.
SHAY	Come out and go riding.
JED	I will.

They clink glasses and down their drinks.

You want another one?

SHAY	No, I should go. Thanks—
JED	Yeah? So soon? Okay. You want me to walk you to your car?
SHAY	No.
JED	Gimme a hug.

They hug. He goes. SHAY is visibly affected by the contact.

Lights change. SHAY and LYLE at home.

SHAY	The entire roof?
LYLE	Got no choice. Has to be done.
SHAY	He should pay for at least half.
LYLE	Not his fault the snow's meltin'.

SHAY	It's his fault he didn't shovel the snow off.
LYLE	He was in the hospital, Shay.
SHAY	So his wife could have called us.
LYLE	Yeah, but me and Hank'll get it done pretty quick. Weather's good. It's no big deal.
SHAY	You're too nice.
LYLE	Hey, how was Group?
SHAY	God, I hate that.
LYLE	What?
SHAY	"Group." Why doesn't anybody say "*the* group"?
LYLE	What's goin' on?
SHAY	Nothing. I'm just tired. Anyway, there was nobody there so Jed and I went for a drink.
LYLE	Oh yeah? How's he doin'?
SHAY	I guess he's all right.
LYLE	How 'bout you?
SHAY	I'm fine.
LYLE	C'mere.

She goes to him.

You feel so good. Let's go ridin', did you see that sky?

SHAY	Go without me. I'm going to take a bath.
LYLE	I want to be with you.

SHAY   So stay.

          She pulls away.

LYLE   How 'bout I join your bath.

SHAY   I'm just going to wash my hair.

LYLE   Okay.

          Lights change. JED, LYLE, *and* LINEE *clapping after Group.*
          SHAY *stands alone.* JED *approaches.*

JED   Still not talking.

SHAY   No.

JED   You're not shy.

SHAY   About some things I am.

          LINEE *comes over.*

LINEE   Big craft show at the high school tomorrow, Shay. Get all your
          Christmas shopping done.

SHAY   It's March.

LINEE   I'm kidding.

SHAY   Oh.

LINEE   We used to go every year, remember? Support the local
          artistes.

SHAY   Right.

LINEE   Do you want to go?

SHAY   Ah…

JED	Christ, not everyone wants a house full of batik and beeswax candles, Linee.
LINEE	Um, was I talking to you?
JED	I'm just saying, not everyone wants to go to every little bake sale in town—
LINEE	It's a craft show, not a bake sale.
JED	What, baked goods aren't crafts?
LINEE	No, they aren't.
JED	I'd be willing to guess there's some bakers out there who'd strongly debate you on that. Some crafty bakers—
LINEE	Jed.
SHAY	Actually, I was thinking about going.
LINEE	You were?
SHAY	I need to get a present for Lois.
LINEE	That's right, she just turned forty. So, do you want to go? Together?
SHAY	Sure.
JED	Crafty crafty.

LYLE re-enters.

LINEE	How 'bout we grab some lunch first and then head on over?
SHAY	All right.
LYLE	You two makin' plans?
LINEE	Yeah, we are.

LYLE	Fantastic. Jedi, gals go shoppin', you and me get choppin'. Getcha back in shape.

He punches him.

JED	I am out of shape.
LINEE	Just don't get drunk and chop your hand off. Lyle, make sure he doesn't hurt himself...
JED	Yeah, yeah.

LINEE and LYLE go out ahead of JED and SHAY.

	After you.
SHAY	Thanks.
JED	Hey.
SHAY	What.
JED	Just hey.

Lights change. LINEE and SHAY at the craft show.

LINEE	I wouldn't say it's a dysfunctional board but they do need some strong leadership pretty badly right now. It's been a couple of years of people coming and going and no real focus or plan for the future. Kind of hemming and hawing over decisions and never really doing what they say they're going to do.
SHAY	Huh.
LINEE	So I just came in and said, "Okay, this is what we're gonna do," and pretty much started to steer everyone in a more focused direction.
SHAY	That's what you do best.

LINEE	Well, I remember we used to do it really well together.
SHAY	Linee…
LINEE	What? Come on, the AGM is coming up in a couple of weeks—
SHAY	I'm not joining any more boards.
LINEE	Why not? You're great at it. This could be exactly what you need.
SHAY	I don't think what I need is really any of your business.
LINEE	You're right. I'm sorry. *(pause)* I'm just glad you're spending time with me. Does it mean I'm forgiven or what?
SHAY	I guess so.
LINEE	That doesn't sound like a yes.
SHAY	We're different people—
LINEE	We're not that different.
SHAY	It's water under the bridge.
LINEE	Okay, you're saying that but—and you're here, so maybe you partly feel that but I still get the feeling you secretly hate me.
SHAY	I just don't think you know how mortifying that was.
LINEE	I know—
SHAY	To have this whole town find out, all our clients—
LINEE	I know—
SHAY	I mean, we chose not to tell people because we didn't want to deal with the gossip and you knew that—

LINEE	I did.
SHAY	You knew it was something I guarded carefully, you knew that Lyle and I didn't want people to know.
LINEE	I know. And I know that we missed out on everything because of it. I mean, J.J. and Carol-Anne would have been like brother and sister and I understand that you're not ready to say her name yet. I wasn't either, a little while ago, but now I think it's important. It's made a huge difference in how I'm coping. It's helping me to keep a connection with J.J. that I didn't think I was allowed to have. I thought I had to bury everything with him—all the memories, all mention of him—but we don't. It's so wrong that we think we have to get over it. Why should we get over it? It's not a secret, it's not this unmentionable thing. *(pause)* And it gets easier. It does. I can't believe how far I've come. I tried to off myself, you know.
SHAY	What?
LINEE	Yup. That's my big secret. Hey, if it'll make you feel any better you can spread it across town if you want. Get me back. Jed doesn't even know.
SHAY	What did you do?
LINEE	I took a bottle of sleeping pills. Obviously not enough. Either that or my stomach's made of Gore-Tex. Woke up, felt like a chisel was chipping away at my skull, puked for about ten hours straight. Passed out again. Woke up. Dry-heaved for another eternity. Slept for three days. It was lovely, I'm telling you.
SHAY	Where was Jed?
LINEE	Who knows? It was the weekend, he was probably going through the exact same thing.
SHAY	What does that mean?

LINEE	He's gotten way worse. His blackouts are really bad. I don't see him from Friday night to Monday morning.
SHAY	How come you put up with that?
LINEE	I'm a sucker.
SHAY	He doesn't seem that bad to me.
LINEE	He's a really good actor.

Pause.

SHAY	I have to go.
LINEE	Okay. I'm so glad we did this. Yay for us. Progress.

Lights change. SHAY.

SHAY	Progress. I see myself progressing. My life passing like miles of road disappearing. I see my skin getting wrinkled, my hair turning white, my breasts sagging and deflating, my ass falling to the floor. I see it all. I see it all without my baby daughter.

Lights change. JED *and* LYLE *at the woodpile.* LYLE *chops.* JED *drinks.*

JED	I don't know, brother. You know what it is? Me and Linee… we're just of a totally different ilk.
LYLE	Ilk?
JED	Yeah, ilk.
LYLE	Ya hunt ilk, dontcha?
JED	Ilk! Ilk—
LYLE	Meat's a little tough. Nice red hide.

JED	Come on, I'm tryna be serious.
LYLE	You gotta work harder, man. You think you're not a good match but you are. You just gotta put a little more effort into keeping her around.
JED	It's a lot more than a little effort, I'm telling you.
LYLE	Linee's a good woman.
JED	Sure she is.

JED crushes his can.

Toss me another beer, brother.

LYLE	That's the sixer.
JED	Is it?

JED counts the cans.

Christ, how'd that happen?

LYLE	You drinkin' more these days or what?
JED	Me? No. No, about the same. I don't know. Maybe a bit more. Not much. Yeah, probably.
LYLE	You got too much time on your hands. Come out and help me with the horses. Get ya busy doin' stuff. Makes ya feel good.
JED	Maybe I should get my own horse.
LYLE	Maybe you should.
JED	Keep him in the garage. No, the kitchen. Better yet, I could keep him in Linee's walk-in closet. That thing is very big. It's big enough to fit a horse. Have to get rid of the shoes. No, the horse could wear 'em!

He laughs at his own joke.

Man, you're lucky. Beautiful land, perfect wife.

LYLE   I already told ya, Shay's a long way from perfect.

JED   You know how many couples don't make it after the death of their kid?

LYLE   We just need more time.

JED   We need… more beer.

LYLE   More beer is what we do not need. You gettin' cold sittin' there in your leather jacket or what?

JED   Nah, I'm toasty. This thing's lined.

LYLE   City boy.

JED   Are you kidding me? I sewed this thing myself. This here's genuine ilk hide.

Lights change. SHAY, LINEE, LYLE, and JED.

SHAY   I kept a box of her little things. Only a box. And I know exactly where it is and what's inside.

LINEE, JED, & LYLE
        I kept:

LYLE   Her blankie.

LINEE   His soother.

JED   His hat.

SHAY   Only a box.

Lights change. SHAY and LYLE at the woodpile.

LYLE	How was the crafty show?
SHAY	Okay.
LYLE	Didja get somethin' for Lois?
SHAY	Uh-huh.
LYLE	How was it hangin' out with Linee?
SHAY	Okay. She told me she tried to kill herself.
LYLE	What?
SHAY	Took a bottle of pills.
LYLE	You serious?
SHAY	She never told anybody.
LYLE	What happened? What did she say?
SHAY	Just that it didn't work. Jed doesn't know. No one knows. And then she found "Group." Now she's all better.
LYLE	Man oh man—
SHAY	I don't feel like cooking dinner tonight.
LYLE	Jesus, I feel so bad we weren't even there for her.
SHAY	I'm going back to the house.
LYLE	We were all goin' through hell and none of us helpin' each other out—
SHAY	I didn't tell you so you could make me feel guilty.
LYLE	I'm not tryin' to make you feel guilty—
SHAY	She betrayed me, Lyle—

LYLE	I know—
SHAY	I was dealing with my own shit—
LYLE	I know you were—
SHAY	I wasn't capable of forgiving her for convenience sake or acting like nothing happened—
LYLE	I know that, all's I'm sayin' is it's unfortunate we couldn't be there for each other—
SHAY	Yes it's unfortunate! It's unfortunate! It's all fucking unfortunate!
LYLE	Shay—
SHAY	I'm going back in.
LYLE	I wanna talk about this.
SHAY	And I don't!
LYLE	Baby, c'mere.
SHAY	No!

Lighting change.

No no no no no. I won't. I can't. Oh God no. I can't do this I can't do it, it's not fair it's not fair. I hate you God I hate you, you fucking bastard I hate you, you fucker, you're a motherfucker, you're a motherfucking sonofabitch bastard I hate your fucking guts I do God I do... I don't wanna be here I don't wanna be here anymore I can't do this I can't do it you asshole why? Why? Why did you take her away she was a baby she was only a baby...

She stops, takes a few breaths and then recovers instantly.

That is what you will not see me do.

Lighting restored.

LYLE   Shayla, c'mere.

            He goes to her and holds her.

            I love you like crazy.

SHAY   Jed.

            JED *appears.*

JED   Yes.

SHAY   Jed.

JED   Yes.

SHAY   Jed...

            Lights to black.

                            REPOSE

Lights up, rockin' music. LINEE, JED, SHAY, and LYLE.

ALL FOUR   Hi, how are you? Fine. Good. Yes, it has. Yup. Thank you. I ap-
             preciate that. Thank you. That's very kind. Hello. Thank you.
             You are, too. Much appreciated. Yes. Thank you. Better. Fine.
             We're hanging in. Thank you. Thank you very much. Thank.
             You. Very. Much.

             Lights change. SHAY and JED at a dance party.

JED   Nice party.

SHAY   No, it isn't.

JED   You're right. *(pause)* You look fantastic.

SHAY   Thank you.

             Pause.

JED   Linee's dancing with Reg Bauer.

SHAY   Reg Bauer. God, he's such an idiot.

JED   Why aren't you dancing?

SHAY   I don't feel like it.

JED   You're a great dancer.

SHAY	I'm not really.
JED	Sure you are. We danced a couple times.
SHAY	We danced that one time on the riverboat—you nearly knocked me over.
JED	I'm what you call a strong leader. Where's Lyle?
SHAY	I don't know. *(pause)* I hate these things.
JED	They're christ-awful.
SHAY	People feel sorry for us, you know.
JED	You think so?
SHAY	I know so.
JED	You're so arrogant. Don't get me wrong, I think it's sexy as hell.
SHAY	Fuck off, Jed.
JED	I think it's spectacular.
SHAY	Why don't you go and dance with your wife?
JED	I'm having fun with you. Admit it. This is fun. Me and you. Come on.
SHAY	You're such a boor.

He laughs.

Stop laughing!

JED	You're allowed to laugh.
SHAY	I can't.

JED	Why, you think you're betraying their memory if you have a good time?
SHAY	So go have a good time.
JED	I never said—
SHAY	Go laugh with the laughers. Go dance.
JED	What—
SHAY	Why are you standing here? Why are you talking to me?
JED	Shayla—
SHAY	Stop calling me that. My husband doesn't even call me that.
JED	It's your name, isn't it?

Pause.

SHAY	You must think I'm such a bitch.
JED	I don't. I think you're amazing.
SHAY	Liar.

Pause.

You were in my dream.

JED	Yeah? What kind of dream was it?
SHAY	We were on a raft.
JED	A raft, huh?
SHAY	In the middle of the ocean. With nothing else around.
JED	What happened?

SHAY	I can't tell you.

JED	Why not? Come on! Okay.

Pause.

SHAY	I was afraid to go to sleep for the longest time. I didn't want to dream.

JED	I dream about J.J. sometimes. We have him back and… and I'll be holding him and… and I can't believe it I can't believe we have him again that he's alive and… I can't understand it I can't get my head around it because I know he's—you know, I know it's not—and I'm trying to enjoy it I'm trying to make the best of it but I just keep thinking, "Isn't he dead? Didn't he die?" I wake up and… I don't know where I am. What's real and what's not… It takes me a couple of minutes to figure out that it didn't really happen.

SHAY	And then what?

JED	I'm relieved.

SHAY	Why?

JED	I don't know.

SHAY	I do.

JED	What?

SHAY	You'd have to be responsible again.

JED	That's a low blow.

SHAY	Am I wrong?

JED	Yeah, you are.

SHAY	Okay. I'm sorry.

Pause.

JED   Tell me your dream.

SHAY   Not here.

LYLE approaches, swingin'.

LYLE   Hey, what are you two kids doin' in this dark little corner, there's a party goin' on—

JED   Yeah, we're being anti-social.

LYLE   Baby, let's dance.

SHAY   Lyle, I don't—

LYLE   I'm not takin' no for an answer.

They dance away. LINEE enters, dancing and flirting.

JED   You and Reg looked like a regular Fred and Ginger out there.

LINEE   Yeah, except he was talking about his truck the whole time.

JED   His big-ass truck.

LINEE   He left it running, unlocked, and some kids took it and smashed it at the bottom of Two Mile Hill.

JED   Kids?

LINEE   Yeah, a buncha fourteen-year-olds.

JED   Anybody get hurt?

LINEE   No. Nobody got hurt.

Lights change. After the dance. JED and LINEE at home. He is still drinking, she is packing.

JED	I know but it's only common goddamn sense in this town to lock yer vehicle and those kids… christ they coulda been killed an' yeah they were bein' stupid but for chrissake you don't leave yer truck runnin' and unlocked for chrissake.
LINEE	Like you've never done that.
JED	I lock it! Come on, I make sure it's locked, for chrissake. I'm pretty sure I don't leave it runnin' unlocked like Reg choice particular fuckin' choice loser Bauer—
LINEE	Oh God, Jed, leave him alone.
JED	I'm just sayin'.
LINEE	God.

He drinks, feeling his gut.

JED	I'm gonna go to the gym tomorrow.
LINEE	I'll believe that when I see it.
JED	Get back inna shape. I don't know why I haven't been going. I love going to the gym. Why the christ don't I just go?
LINEE	Because you set unrealistic expectations for yourself, then you get all disappointed when you don't meet them and then you give up.
JED	It was a rhetorical question.
LINEE	Of course it was.
JED	I lost my good shape ever since not bein' with Lyle alla time. You see how gooda shape he's in?
LINEE	He works outside all the time, what do you expect?
JED	I really let myself down. I mean, I really let myself go. You should see Lyle, he's built like a brick shithouse for chrissake.

LINEE	I have seen him.
JED	What d'ya mean?
LINEE	What do you mean, what do I mean? I've seen Lyle's body.
JED	When the christ have you seen Lyle's body?
LINEE	When the hell do you think? Practically every weekend we ever went to the hot springs with them or camping or hiking—
JED	All right, all right.
LINEE	Stop comparing yourself to Lyle.
JED	I'm gonna start goin' again regularly like I use to and I'm gonna get back inna shape. I'm gonna go every day and get back inna shape—
LINEE	*(overlapping)* How about instead of saying you'll go every day and then getting all disappointed in yourself when you don't, try getting up and saying, "I'm going to the gym today." Then you won't have to change your entire musculature to look like Lyle's, you'll just be going for a workout because you want to and because it feels good—
JED	*(overlapping)* I was goin' regularly before Christmas. I was goin' every single day and then I got that cold, for chrissake, right after New Year's and then I had to go Down South—
LINEE	That was two months ago—
JED	I haven't had time! Christ, between work and everything else—
LINEE	And then you get mad at me—
JED	I jus' needa get back inna routine for chrissake, I know that about m'self 'cause if I have a routine I'm good I can stay on track with a system, i's jus' needing a system tha's all a system that'll remind me or like if I had like a trainer or something—

LINEE	You had a trainer.
JED	The thing is about that is, see, it wasn't working but if I jus' do what I need ta do then I'll do it, and the thing I never unnerstood is why Lyle doesn't ever seem to have this problem. Y'know? He keeps in shape, he does the trips, he enjoys himself and he doesn't even haveta think about it, he just does it.
LINEE	Stop putting him up on a pedestal. Lyle lost his daughter just like you lost your son—
JED	Not lost. Not christing lost!
LINEE	Fine.

He drinks. He finally notices her packing.

JED	What are you doing?
LINEE	I'm packing.
JED	Here we go. Aw christ, Linee.
LINEE	I'm going down to visit my sister on Friday. I told you that.
JED	Why the christ are you packing now?
LINEE	Because I like to be organized.
JED	It's a week away for chrissake.
LINEE	Would you please just… go and sleep in the den. God! I'm so tired of this!
JED	What'd I say? Hey.

He tries to touch her. She pushes him away.

| LINEE | Stop it, Jed! |

There is a sip or two of drink left in his glass and he flings the liquid at her. She leaves. He lifts his drink in her direction.

JED   Sweet dreams!

        Lights change. SHAY *and* LINEE *in* LINEE'S *car. A magnificent view.*

LINEE   Everything's melting.

        Silence.

        Remember when you first brought me here? I couldn't believe it. That you could drive two minutes out of town and see this. Thanks for indulging me.

SHAY   Thanks for driving me home.

LINEE   I used to bring Jed Jr. here a lot. Mostly to get away from Jed if things had gotten bad again. I'd be at my breaking point and I'd come here with him. Sometimes I'd think about driving off the cliff. I mean I never would have done it, I just kind of saw it in my head. J.J. was just starting to talk. Saying words that weren't words. His own little language. Once, this eagle flew right over the car. Swooped down really close it was incredible. J.J. screamed, he was so excited. Now... when I see an eagle, I think... not that it's J.J. but... that he's okay. *(pause)* Do you have things like that? Things that make you think Carol-Anne is all right?

SHAY   No.

LINEE   Hm.

        Silence.

SHAY   Sometimes I think... there's this guy I see around town, this old Indian guy. Once he was making her smile when we were in line buying groceries, just making funny faces at her and stuff. When I see him around I think... I don't know.

LINEE	What?
SHAY	I don't know. It just reminds me.
LINEE	It's like a message, isn't it?
SHAY	Can we go?
LINEE	Oh, sure…
SHAY	Sorry. I've been trying to ignore this pain in my head—
LINEE	Shay, why didn't you tell me you had a headache?

Lights change.

SHAY	Because if I say anything, I will ask about him.

Lights change. SHAY and LYLE in the den. SHAY is watching TV.

LYLE	Come on, can't you just agree that it's helpin' us a little bit?
SHAY	I think it's making things worse.
LYLE	Worse? How?
SHAY	It's giving me headaches, I'm more depressed than I've ever been—
LYLE	You gotta give it some more time.
SHAY	I've given it almost two months—
LYLE	They say to give it three—
SHAY	Who? Who says?
LYLE	The people who've been goin' long enough to know—
SHAY	Do you think they know me better than I know myself? I know when I'm getting worse and I'm telling you it's sinking

me deeper into a hole and maybe it's helping you and that's fine. I'm not telling you to stop going but it's not helping me. It's not. And you know... I feel like you're forcing me to get over it faster or—

LYLE   I'm not doin' that—

SHAY   Or I can feel your expectations of me. I can feel you wanting something from me and I can feel your disappointment because I'm not giving it—

LYLE   I'm not disappointed. I'm tryna close this gap that's come between us—

SHAY   You want me to get to where Linee is or where you are, you want me to read the books and go through the five stages or the seven or whatever and I'm not you, Lyle, I can't just look at the time we had with her and be grateful for it—

LYLE   I'm not askin' you to do that.

SHAY   But you are. You want me to see the silver lining, you want me to get to that place where I'm feeling thankful—

LYLE   I don't want you to do anythin' you don't wanna do.

SHAY   So what if I want to watch TV every night for the rest of my life? What if I never want another kid? You say that but you don't mean it, Lyle.

LYLE   Okay, yes, I want you to let me back in. I do. You've closed the door on me and... and, yeah, I'm maybe pushin' on it a little too hard sometimes because it's not even open a crack, y'know? I can't even get it open just a little anymore to even start talkin' about any of this stuff—and this is good right now, it's good we're talkin' now because even just to hear you say that you feel like I'm pushin' you or you feel like I have expectations a-you to be more positive or whatever is good. It is. Because we gotta talk about it—

SHAY   But I do not want to talk about it!

LYLE	No, you don't! So what do you think, Shay? That stayin' shut down is gonna keep bad things from happenin'? You lock up your heart so it doesn't get broken? Ya cut me off, ya cut yerself off… you think that's what life is all about? Tryin' to make sure you never have to feel anything again? Ya think ya can avoid the pain? Let me tell you something, we are gonna die. We are. And livin' pretendin' like I'm not is no life for me. I don't know why I'm alive today and she isn't. I don't know why. But I am. We're still here. And we gotta make what we can of all this, of what we got left. What the hell else is the point?

She goes back to the TV.

SHAY	I'm not going back.

The lights change. JED and SHAY in his car.

Thanks for the lift.

JED	Sure. Anytime.
SHAY	I'm supposed to get my car back tomorrow.
JED	Lucky I ran into you.
SHAY	I would've taken a cab.
JED	That's an expensive cab ride.
SHAY	Doesn't matter. *(pause)* Lyle's in the Junction.
JED	Ah.

Silence.

SHAY	I'm stuck.
JED	Stuck…
SHAY	I can't seem to get out of the car.

JED	That's okay.
	Silence.
SHAY	Jed.
JED	Yes?
SHAY	Never mind.
JED	What?
SHAY	Do you think they were real?
JED	Who?
SHAY	They.
JED	The kids? Do I think they were real? As opposed to what? Aliens?
SHAY	Don't joke.
JED	What… okay. Do I think they were real. Ah… yes?
SHAY	Why do you think they were born?
JED	I don't know.
SHAY	Linee believes there's a Higher Plan.
JED	Yuh. She does.
SHAY	I wish I did. God, I'm so weak.
JED	You're not weak. Come on. You're not weak. I admire how strong you are.
SHAY	You're so wrong about me.
JED	Shayla—sorry. I keep calling you that.

SHAY   I don't mind.

JED   Why did you tell me you did?

             She looks at him. He looks back.

SHAY   I have to feed the dogs.

JED   You have to feed the dogs.

SHAY   Yes, I have to feed the dogs.

JED   Okay.

SHAY   Okay.

JED   So…

SHAY   God, I'm being bad.

JED   So what?

SHAY   I'm acting like a teenager!

JED   I like teenagers—I don't mean I *like* teenagers—

SHAY   Jed.

JED   Tell me your dream.

SHAY   It was hot.

JED   Okay. Hot. What—

SHAY   We were fucking.

JED   Oh yeah?

SHAY   I sucked you off.

JED   Huh.

SHAY	Yeah.
JED	Wow.
SHAY	Satisfied?
JED	You tell me.
	They laugh.
	I like it when you laugh.
	He touches her.
SHAY	I don't want to do this.
JED	Okay. You don't—
SHAY	I don't.
JED	Okay—
SHAY	Tell me to get out of the car. Right now. Say it. "Shayla, get out of the car."
JED	I don't want you to get out of the car.
SHAY	Please. Just. Say it.
JED	No.
SHAY	God.
JED	What.
SHAY	Fuck.
JED	Yeah.
	They kiss.

SHAY   Fuck—

JED   Uh-huh—

They kiss harder. JED's phone rings. They pull apart.

Wait— Hello?... Linee, I'm ah... No, I ran into Peter, he needed a lift home... What?... Oh, christ I forgot... I'm sorry, I'll... Okay, I'm coming.

A look. Lights change. LYLE is chopping wood.

LYLE   She's workin' through it, she is. She's gotta do it her own way, she always has. Yer mom's a strong woman and it comes across as pride and stubbornness sometimes but it's only 'cause she's scared. We just gotta keep lovin' her. She's gonna come around to us, Carol-Anne. We just gotta keep makin' sure she knows how much we love her. So, if ya can, just let her know you're okay. Just let her know that she can still talk to ya, that ya haven't gone nowhere and yer still her girl. Just let 'er know somehow.

Lights change. LINEE and JED in their home. LINEE at the door waving goodbye to their guests.

LINEE   Don't get pulled over, Jake! Bye, Sue!

JED is pouring another drink.

Jed, can you please not pour that? I want to talk to you.

JED   I can't have a drink while you talk?

LINEE   You've already had half the bottle and I want to talk about this before you go past your limit—

JED   Go ahead.

LINEE   Can you please just wait until we're finished—

He slams down his glass.

Thank you.

JED	What is it?
LINEE	I'm not your secretary.
JED	Christ, what do you want from me, Linee?
LINEE	I want to have a conversation—
JED	It's not a conversation you want, it's a confrontation, you're gonna lecture me and what you really want is for me to sit here and take it.
LINEE	Jed, do you like me?
JED	What?
LINEE	Do. You. Like. Me.
JED	What kind of christ-ass stupid question is that?
LINEE	Because tonight when we were waiting for you and one more time I found myself wondering if you were going to show up and if you did would you embarrass yourself—
JED	Yeah, yeah—
LINEE	I suddenly had a moment of clarity. I mean a real moment of absolute clarity.
JED	That's great!
LINEE	I realized that no matter how hard I try, no matter what I do for you or even for myself for that matter, you are never really going to like me. And I am never really going to like you either. Oh, yeah, we fell in love. We had a honeymoon romance but that's just what it was. It was a… a short-lived fantasy. And when it wore off we were two strangers trying to force ourselves to get along.
JED	That's the definition of a relationship, for christ sake.

LINEE   It's like I irritate you all the time. I can feel it, it's like I grate on your nerves and the only time you show me any tenderness is when you're loaded—

JED   What about me? When was the last time you showed me any kind of anything, huh?

LINEE   Do you think you're attractive when you're like this?

JED   What do you want from me!

LINEE   Even if Jed Jr. had lived I don't think it could have saved us.

JED   Just shit or get off the pot already—

LINEE   What did you say to me?

JED   I said, have the guts to say what it is you really want to say.

LINEE   You want me to say it? I want out.

          He makes the sound of a fanfare.

JED   Ta-da! She said it!

          He does a crude little shuffle.

LINEE   Look at you.

          She leaves. He drinks. Lights change. LYLE and LINEE at Group.

LYLE   It's hard that my wife's not here, that she doesn't want to come anymore but... I dunno. I can't make it better for her, y'know? I just wanna be able to save her from havin' to go through it and... and I... I don't know how not to want to, y'know? *(pause)* I almost didn't come tonight, y'know? But I don't wanna do that. I'm learnin' somethin' here. Even if I don't know what it is just yet. So. Yeah. That's all I got. Thanks for listenin'.

They clap.

LINEE   I left my husband last night and I'm… *(laughs)* Sorry, I'm not laughing because it's funny ~~I just can't…~~ I just can't believe those are the words that just came out of my mouth. "I left my husband." Yeah, God, it feels like a joke, ~~I can't believe it.~~ I keep thinking I'm dreaming but no… I'm awake! I think I'm in shock or something… I must be, I don't know and yet I feel really grounded it's really weird. *(pause)* Yeah, I moved into a hotel and I got there and it occurred to me that I've never been on my own before. Never. ~~I've been alone in my marriage and you know I've been in a long-distance relationship and stuff but I've never not been in a relationship.~~ And that is just crazy because it means that since I was, like, thirteen I've just gone from boyfriend to boyfriend and then married my husband and… ~~really it's been so hard to let go of J.J. and stay in denial about my marriage.~~ It's like… I can finally see myself. *(pause)* I'm terrified. I don't know what's going to happen. But I'm excited too. I am. I don't know what for, just… yeah. *(pause)* I have this picture of Jed Jr. and I put it on the mirror in my hotel room and… and I know a big part of me staying with Jed was not wanting to break his little heart but… he understands. I know he does. *(pause)* Anyway I just wanted to say thanks. I'm going Down South to visit my sister for a while and… yeah. Thanks everybody.

   They clap. Lights change. SHAY *alone, watching television, masturbating through her clothes.* LYLE *enters.*

LYLE   Shay?

   She freezes.

   Whatcha watchin'?

SHAY   I don't even know. How was… Group?

LYLE   Jed and Linee split up.

SHAY   Oh my God.

LYLE	She left him.
SHAY	What happened?
LYLE	I didn't really talk to her. She was talkin' to Sue afterward and I dunno, she just shared that she left and she's stayin' in one of the hotels—
SHAY	I'll call her.
LYLE	That'd be good.
SHAY	Have you talked to Jed?
LYLE	Went lookin' for him downtown. He's not in his usual spots. Linee asked me to take her to the airport tomorrow. She's going Down South.
SHAY	I can take her.
LYLE	Okay. Hey, we can do this. You and me. We're gonna make it. Okay?
SHAY	'Kay.

Lights change. SHAY *and* LINEE *at the airport.*

LINEE	He's gonna die without me, that's what scares me the most. He's gonna pass out in his own puke if I'm not there to roll him over. I really thought Group could help him. But he just didn't want me to leave.

Silence.

SHAY	You should go through.
LINEE	I can't wait to smell the cherry blossoms and walk on the beach.
SHAY	We're never going to see you again.

LINEE	You never know. *(pause)* I can't tell you how happy I am that you called me. That you wanted to see me off.

LINEE goes to give SHAY a hug.

SHAY	Linee, I ah… I… I'm ah… having… a really hard time right now—
LINEE	Oh honey—
SHAY	No it's okay but… I just wanted to tell you that… I've been… ah—
LINEE	It's okay—
SHAY	I've been such a bitch to you—
LINEE	You don't have to say anything—
SHAY	I do though and I appreciate you for… for your kindness and your forgiveness… you're really a much better person than I am—
LINEE	I am not—
SHAY	You are, you don't know what I am—
LINEE	Shay, you're being way too hard on yourself—
SHAY	Yeah, well there's a reason for that. Anyway… I just wanted you to know that… there were so many times… I wanted to call you. I just… I could never bring myself to pick up the phone.

Pause.

LINEE	Thank you.
SHAY	You need to go.

LINEE holds out her arms. They hug. SHAY lets go. LINEE holds on. SHAY hugs tighter. LINEE heads off. Lights change. SHAY working in the barn. JED approaches. He's loaded.

JED   Here you are.

SHAY   Jesus! You scared me.

JED   Sorry.

SHAY   What are you doing here?

JED   You called me.

SHAY   No, I didn't.

JED   Call display doesn't lie.

SHAY   I'm busy right now.

JED   I came out to see Lyle.

SHAY   He's not here.

JED   What's wrong with you?

SHAY   Nothing.

           Pause.

JED   Linee get off okay?

SHAY   Yes.

JED   So what's up?

SHAY   I'm—nothing. What do you mean?

JED   I mean why'd you call me?

SHAY   To see how you were.

JED	I'm good.
SHAY	Your wife just left you.
JED	Okay so I'm shit.

She gets away from him.

Shayla—

SHAY	I've been meaning to talk to you—
JED	I thought you'd been meaning not to talk to me.
SHAY	What did you think was going to happen?
JED	I thought maybe I'd hear from you a little sooner.
SHAY	I've been busy.
JED	Huh. So… you want to go for a drive?
SHAY	I can't right now.
JED	So why'd you call me?
SHAY	I told you.
JED	To see how I'm doing.
SHAY	Yes.
JED	And… okay.
SHAY	You're okay?
JED	I'm okay. I'm great. Hey, thanks for the concern.
SHAY	Jed.
JED	What.

SHAY   I am concerned.

JED   You are, huh?

            He touches her.

SHAY   Don't.

JED   Why not?

SHAY   It doesn't feel right.

JED   It felt right before.

            He pulls her to him.

SHAY   That was before.

JED   So what's changed?

            She pulls away.

SHAY   I'm working, I'm busy—

JED   So take a break.

SHAY   I don't want to.

JED   Why?

SHAY   I just… let's just forget it.

JED   I don't want to forget it.

SHAY   Well, you're going to have to.

JED   You're the one that started it—

SHAY   I started it?

JED   Yeah, christ. You're incredibly full of shit, you know that?

| SHAY | I'm sorry. I'm very sorry. I lost my mind. |
| JED | You lost your mind. Christ. |

He pulls out a flask. Drinks.

| SHAY | I think you should go home now. |
| JED | Can I just have a hug? Please? Please. |

She hesitates, then gives him a hug. Their affection turns hot. They start to kiss, going at it, grinding and getting hotter. They drop to the ground. He's fumbling with his belt, the ground beneath her is uncomfortable. It's not working. He's desperate. She's disgusted. Finally, she pushes him off her, crawls away.

| SHAY | Go home, Jed. |
| JED | Yeah. |

He leaves. She cries. Lights change. LINEE is Down South.

| LINEE | Yesterday, I went for a walk on the beach. It's not a nice beach or anything, there's a big factory right there and tons of rusted-out boats in the water and industrial-type junk everywhere, it's like an environmental disaster zone. But if you walk in a certain direction you can't see any of it, it's all behind you. You just see this pristine stretch of rocky beach and a thick cedar wood that heads out to the point and then the big water beyond. It was really early. I hadn't slept and I was feeling like crap and regretting everything and hearing all these voices in my head telling me I'm a piece of shit and I should go back. I was feeling crazy, complete insanity and... then I saw this eagle. At the top of this tree lifting its wings as though it was going to take off but then not and... without even realizing it I started whispering to it just... saying "Hello" and "Look at you" and... then it let go and started flying toward me... swooping down right above me then it flew straight up, beating the air and making it whistle, the sound of his name. |

Lights change. SHAY *on their deck in a bathrobe, staring at the mountains.* LYLE *enters.*

LYLE   Baby, I couldn't find ya.

SHAY   You found me.

LYLE   Yer not in front of the TV.

SHAY   No. I'm outside. It's still light out.

LYLE   Did you feed the horses?

SHAY   Yeah, but the donkey wouldn't come. I don't know where he is.

LYLE   I'll go find him.

SHAY   Wait. Come keep me warm.

LYLE   I'm all dirty.

SHAY   I don't care.

LYLE   Yer all clean.

SHAY   C'mere.

He wraps his arms around her.

LYLE   Yer freezin'.

SHAY   We just lost the sun.

LYLE   Come inside and warm up.

SHAY   You're warm.

LYLE   Mm. You smell great.

She kisses him.

SHAY	I missed you.
LYLE	I missed you, too.
	They kiss.
	Baby?
SHAY	Yeah…
LYLE	Did somethin' happen?
SHAY	Let's go inside.
	She tries to pull him inside.
LYLE	Wait, did Jed show up yet?
	She stops, letting go of him.
SHAY	What?
LYLE	He left a message askin' if I was gonna be home. Did he come out here? *(pause)* Shay? Was he here? Hello? Can you look at me please?
SHAY	No, I can't.
LYLE	Why not?
	He waits.
	What the fuck is going on?
	She meets his eyes. He gets it.
	What? Fuck. Okay.
SHAY	Lyle—
LYLE	No, I'm goin' to find George Clooney—

SHAY	Wait—
LYLE	No, I got it. I get it.
SHAY	Lyle, I love you.
LYLE	Yeah. I love you, too.

He leaves. Lights change. JED *in the bar.*

JED See the important thing to remember is this, and I always say this because it is… it's the most important thing to remember and that is—because you can lose sight of it so easily you have it and then it's gone, like "bing," and you've lost it but if you can remember it, if you can remember how important it is then you know, you know that… that… that…

Lights change. SHAY *and* LYLE *in bed. Long silence.*

LYLE You know that scar on my leg? The one on the inside-a my thigh? Broken branch punctured a perfect hole in my skin size of a dime. No blood, no rip in my clothes. Nothin'. Mom couldn't figure out why I was screamin' so loud. Then she took everythin' off me and there it was. Punctured a hole in the skin just like paper. *(pause)* Sometimes a thing can hurt so much, y'know? But you can't see what's makin' it hurt. And then ya see it… ya see what's actually makin' it hurt and… and it doesn't make it hurt any less but… now maybe you know why. *(pause)* Y'know, I always told you this. I told you I'd die if I lost ya. But I wouldn't, y'know? I wouldn't. So if you wanna leave me, well… you need to do that.

He waits. She turns to face him.

SHAY I'm not going to leave you.

Lights change. LYLE *and* SHAY *at Group. They clap.* SHAY *raises her hand.*

I'll go. *(pause)* I don't really know what to say, it's… the first time I've spoken… here. I've wanted to before… break those... those long moments of silence... I can't stand the silence. But I can't stand not saying anything anymore either. I've been afraid that if I talk... I wouldn't be able to bear it. But I can't bear it now. *(pause)* I'm not the person I want to be. I've done things I... regret so deeply and... I think I'm really sick. But I don't know how to change. So... I thought I'd say something and... really it's that... I just... I miss my baby. I miss my little girl. I loved her so much. She was... her name was... Carol-Anne. Her name was Carol-Anne.

LYLE *puts his hand on her leg. She puts her hands on his hand.*

Blackout.

Acknowledgements

Thank you to Moira Sauer, Kelly Thornton, all the Jeds and the Lyles, to the designers, musicians, and the crew guys and gals. Thank you to Sour Brides' Board of Directors and big thanks to the individual donors, sponsors, and presenters.

Thank you to Yukon Tourism and Culture (Touring Artist Fund), Lotteries Yukon (Yukon Arts Funding, Advanced Artist Award), Yukon Arts Fund, and the Canada Council for the Arts.

Grateful acknowledgement to the babies, real and imagined.

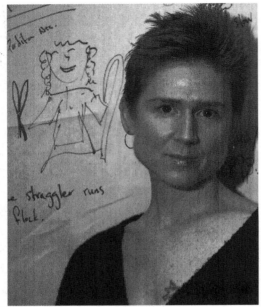

Author photo © Bruce Barrett

Celia McBride is an award-winning writer/performer whose work as a theatre artist and filmmaker has reached audiences all across Canada as well as in Europe and the United States. In 1995 Celia won the Fox Fellowship Award and travelled to Ireland where her play *Choke My Heart* was produced in 1998. In 2001 Celia was commissioned by the Stratford Festival of Canada to write a play for the inaugural season of the Studio Theatre where *Walk Right Up* subsequently premiered in 2002. Her artistic practice has expanded to include a coaching and workshop facilitation business called Inspiring Works (www.celiamcbride.com) and she was the artistic director of the Yukon cultural segment for the Victory Ceremonies at the Vancouver 2010 Olympics. Celia is the co-artistic director of Sour Brides Theatre (www.sourbrides.com), a member of the Playwrights Guild of Canada, and a graduate of the National Theatre School of Canada. She lives in Whitehorse, Yukon, where she was born and spent her earliest years.